Borning In and Borning Out

Written and Illustrated by

Marnie Muller, MLA

HEARTWISDOM
PUBLISHERS

You and the Universe® Series

BORNING IN AND BORNING OUT
BY MARNIE MULLER, MLA

ISBN 978-0-692-58089-9
1. All Ages   2. Spirituality   3. Psychology   4. Body, Mind & Spirit   5. Death & Dying

Layout and cover design by Susan L. Yost

Thanks to all who shared their wisdom...

Once upon a time
when the gate of birth opened...

and you came **borning in**
to our planet Earth

you brought with you

...inside of you...

a picture of the entire universe!

Amazing...

So the entire universe comes with you
...as an essence within you

and the entire universe

    ...as an essence within you...

takes in all you experience

    throughout your life

...and brings it together within itself.
Amazing...

Yes, inside of you
there is a special place
where your heart is floating

and that special place
    holds all you take with you
on your journey
        of soul and spirit.
                Amazing...

And as you live your life
...through all your adventures
and challenges...

you are actually

giving back to the universe

all of who you are

and what you do.

So when you are

surprised by a butterfly

or

follow a bee

or

climb a tree...

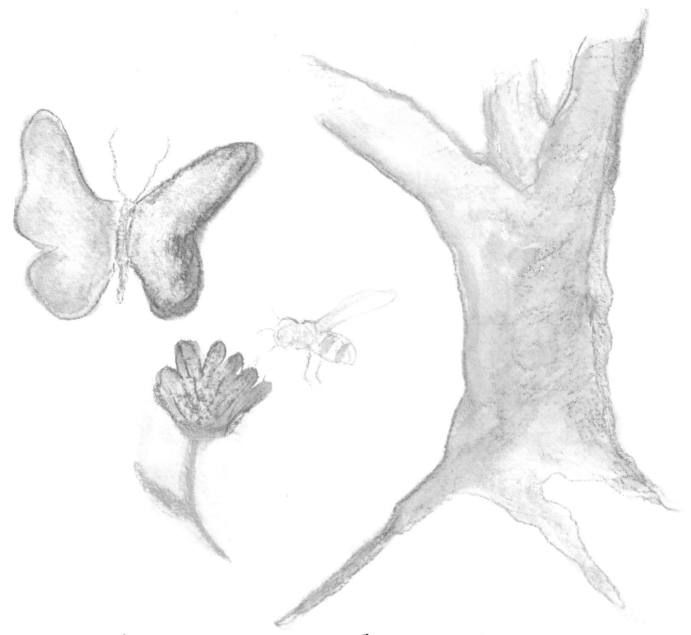

your feelings and findings
      are your gifts to the universe

And because only you are you...
there will be "aha" moments
that only you can experience
in your own way...

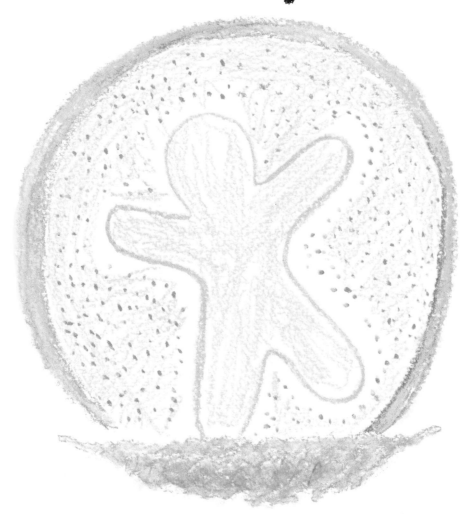

and each "aha" becomes a gift
to the entire universe.
Amazing...

Have you ever wondered how you fit in with **ALL** that is?

hmm m m hm m

The universe may seem very huge with its stars and planets and galaxies...

You, though, are in the midst of it all.

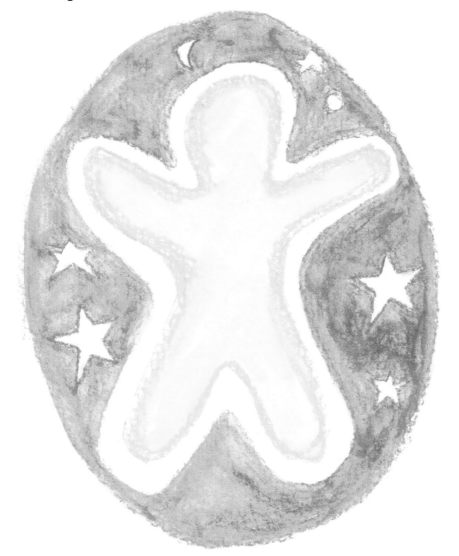

You are at the very center of the
universe from where you stand

...and inside of you
is the heart of all there is,
Great and small.

Only you can greet
the rest of the universe
from the place where you stand.

Only you can sing the song back
to the universe that comes from
the special place within you.

Being aware of all this
and the special place inside you
where your heart is floating...

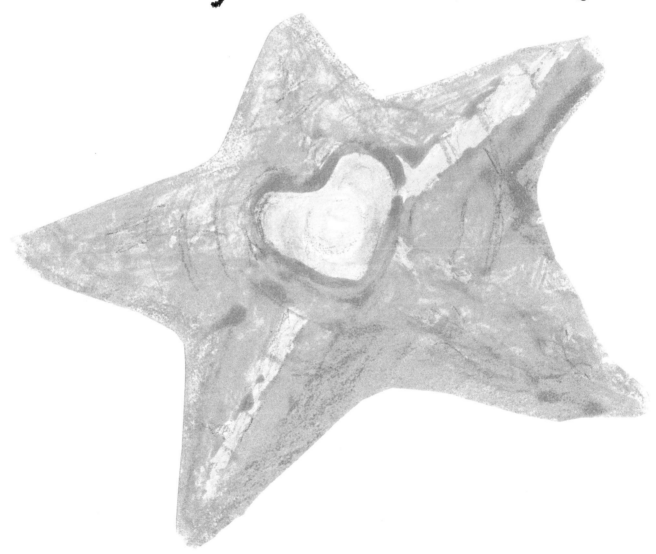

you know how it feels
    to be you in universe
        ...and universe in you.

Each day as you awaken you enjoy being aware that you ARE aware...

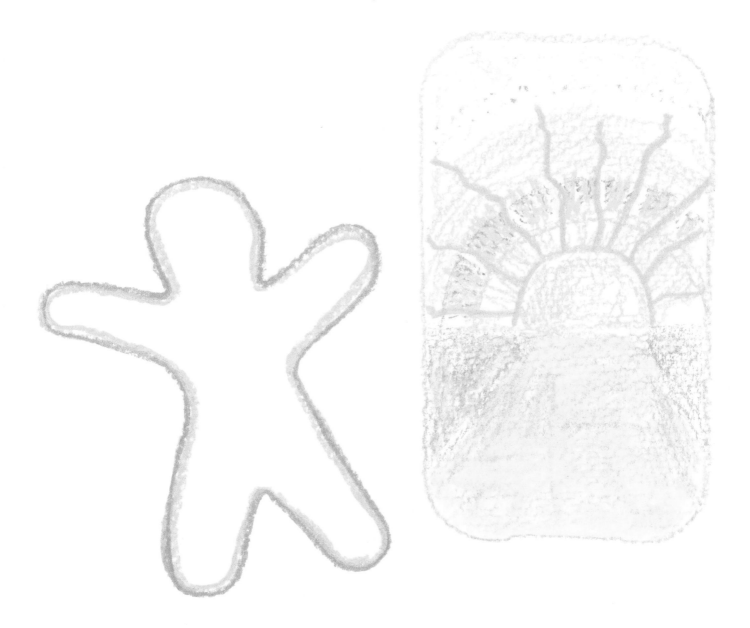

and each day you remember your own life journey and its essence.

So then, when it's time to pass through the gate of borning out

...of returning...

ALL you have
learned
is then
drawn
together
into that
special
place
that
surrounds
your heart.

That special place within you holds all you are taking with you on your journey of soul and spirit.

And as you expand...
　　　　ever more widely in the Spirit

You then share with the universe
all you have learned...
and all you have done.
Amazing...

For the substance of the entire
universe is there held within you...

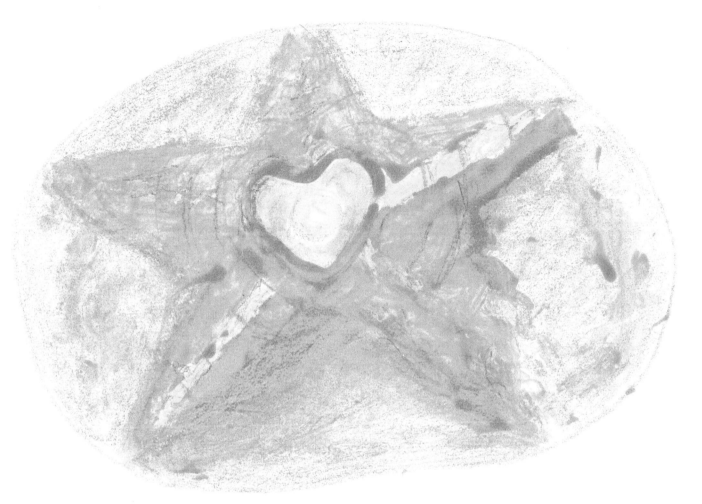

It came from the universe
        and was gathered up
    into that special place within you,
as an essence in your heart

and now

it begins
to return...

to go back
home...

into the
universe...

once more...

Amazing!

CPSIA information can be obtained
at www.ICGtesting.com
Printed in the USA
LVOW05s1448061016

507695LV00033B/203/P

9 780692 580899